Get Orga

GW01035779

Your 12 Month Home Clutter Killer Guide

Colette Leigh

DEDICATION

To my husband, children and friends – thank you so much for your support, patience and pestering!

TABLE OF CONTENTS

INTRODUCTION

Thank you so much for buying my first book.

My name is Colette Leigh, and I'm a busy wife and mother of three children, two Labradors and a work at home husband, and we live in wonderful Wyoming.

According to friends and family, I'm rather good at keeping our home tidy and organized. It just feels natural to me, but after considerable pestering, I've finally been convinced to put my ideas down on paper, and into this book. I've gone to great lengths explaining the routines and techniques I use every day to keep our home tidy, decluttered and consequently stress free.

I hope you enjoy it, and I am sure it will make a positive difference to your life and your home.

Best wishes,

Colette

1

YOUR 12 MONTH HOME ORGANIZATION PLAN

Organizing a cluttered house can be an overwhelming ordeal. No matter where you turn everywhere just seems so messy. From the closet to the garage, both are usually jam-packed. The worst part is that despite the chaos, the clutter seems to be piling up! To avoid going crazy, you'll simply need to create a plan.

Your plan will guarantee results if you **believe** that it can work.

This is possible by dividing a large cleaning project into small manageable tasks. You can make a plan for each month of the year. You don't necessarily have to wait until the end of each month; you can always do a few tasks in advance.

First Month: Your Bedroom

It's best to start with the bedroom since it is the most personal room in your house. It's where you spend most of your life and take the opportunity to connect with your partner. When you de-clutter your bedroom, you'll feel a whole lot better and it can even help you sleep and wake more refreshed.

Start by creating three separate piles for the moveable items that are in your bedroom. The three piles should be distinguished as follows: to keep, donate and throw out. You can easily divide your bedroom into manageable tasks if you find it's too much to handle in one day or weekend. You can also separate by space such as: closet, dresser, under the bed, etc.

Second Month: Master Bathroom

You'll need to create labels and buy storage containers before you start any cleaning here. When you've done this, go to the medicine cabinet and look under the bathroom sink. Remove all the clutter in these areas by placing them in the storage containers. Use the labels for items that you don't necessary want to throw out, but think it's better to find another location for.

Third Month: Your Kitchen

The kitchen is by far one of the most challenging areas in any home. You'll be amazed how many extra utensils you have that you're really not using. When you start your cleaning you'll need to repeat the keep, donate and throw out process mentioned above, to de-clutter your kitchen. When you're finished, every item must have its individual space. If you manage to do this, then you'll be amazed at just how light your kitchen feels.

Fourth Month: Reassess

The fourth month is when you'll reassess your cleaning process in the main areas you've covered already. Items that are misplaced should be re-organized and any extra unnecessary clutter should be tossed out. Look out for appliances and furniture that aren't working and fix or dispose of them.

You can start your reassessment by doing the bedroom first and then moving onto the bathroom and kitchen.

Fifth Month: Guest Bedroom / Home Office

If you don't use your guest room/home office that often, then chances are there is very little to clean. The occasional dusting and de-cluttering however can be very helpful to make these areas nice and tidy. Remove unused items from your guest bedroom and look under the bed for fallen things. If you use your home office to store small items, then assess just how necessary they are and repeat the keep, donate and throw out process.

Sixth Month: Children's Bedrooms

Your children's bedroom can be a battlefield to clean, so you'll need to prepare yourself! Scattered toys, clothes, food, dirty drink glasses and dishes are usually the main culprits that you'll need to dig through. Chances are your children have outgrown some of their clothes and there will be lot of items that you'll need to donate or just toss out.

Get your children involved when you're de-cluttering their room. This will take some burden off you and teach them about being responsible. If you find many items that can be donated, then prepare a garage sale. You'll be surprised just how much your child may love the idea - especially if there is some monetary reward involved!

Seventh Month: Additional Bathrooms

It's quite common for some homes to have additional bathrooms. If this is your case, then go through each extra bathroom to see which items you can keep, donate and toss out. Look behind the bathroom sink and in the shower for scattered items. Organize shampoos, makeup, and any other items you encounter.

Eighth Month: Relax!

Use the eighth month to relax. During this time you can plan the garage sale mentioned above if you haven't already done so. You can also use the time to reassess your progress and evaluate which areas in your house need additional cleaning. If you find anything else that isn't working, then fix it, throw it out or save it for the garage sale. You would be surprised how many broken or faulty everyday items that some people will buy, knowing that they are broken, or for spares or repairs.

Ninth Month: Garage

The garage is one of those areas that usually get very little attention when it comes to every day cleaning. As a result, you'll find that when you finally start that there is a **lot** of junk to take care of. This is because most people just haphazardly pack things in the garage just to get them out of their way. If you're one of these, then you'll need to use the whole month to organize the garage. You may find that it'll be necessary to use all your weekends in the month to make the organization process worthwhile.

Tenth Month: Family / Living Room

The family/living room is a rather personal location for many people, because this is where all of the family comes together to share time. Scattered books, toys and unused items are quite common in these areas. Simply look around the room to find everything that is out of place. Organize using the three process mentioned above. Get the family involved also, so that the next time there is a family get-together everyone will be more careful with what they do and leave behind.

Eleventh Month: Dining Room and Additional Rooms You Haven't Dealt With

People that have a big house with a lot of space may have extra rooms that can become cluttered. The dining room is not difficult to clean, but it can become messy with spilled food. Get a broom, mop and other cleaning agents to work through the room. Take some time to think about rearranging also to maximize space and change the feel of the room.

Twelfth Month: Basement and / or Attic

These are also forgotten areas that can get overlooked as time passes. However, this won't be a demanding challenge if you use the three-tier process mentioned above when organizing. You'll need to get storage baskets to ensure that everything is kept in the ideal place. Depending on the extent of the clutter, you'll only need a weekend or as much as a month to organize everything. When you are finished you'll realize just how organized and clean your house is. The best part is that it'll be clutter free!

2

TOP FIVE CLUTTER KILLERS

C lutter lowers the quality of life you have in any environment, the disorganization potentially adding to every day stress. Luckily, despite the challenge, you can use these marvelous methods to gain control and get rid of clutter forever.

#1 Clutter Collector

When things are left out of place, then clutter starts to become a big problem. To avoid this, you'll need a clutter collector to temporarily store all these items, until you are ready to put them where they belong. Find a good sized container, plastic or otherwise, that you can carry with you from room to room – this will be your clutter collector! This is a very simple process and you'll be surprised at just how easy it can be after walking through your living space. Do this at the end of the day for five minutes and you'll soon have a house that is clutter free.

There will come a point where your clutter collector becomes full. But you really don't want to wait until then do you? To avoid this, spend at least five minutes putting the things back where they belong. You don't have to bear this burden alone either: simply ask each member of your family to be more responsible when leaving things around the house. If your gentle push doesn't work, then calling them one by one each day to help arrange things should do the trick. They'll eventually get tired of cleaning up after themselves and will do so naturally, as they go about their day. You on the other hand will get a little well-deserved rest!

#2 Get Rid of Ten Useless Things

You can nearly make a game of this (well, almost!) to make the whole process of clutter removal a little more enticing. You've got to get rid of ten items in any room. Just choose any room, and from there choose ten things you really don't need, to throw away or donate. Limit this list of items to ten. Do this every day for five minutes until you are left with valuable items that you actually have enough room for and really, really want.

#3 Utilize Double Function Furniture

Clutter becomes a nuisance when many items compete for the little space you have. However, even if you don't have a large space, then you can still store clutter away in furniture that is specially made with extra compartments. Take the coffee and end table in your room for example. These can double as chests or have extra drawers for storage to place other things that you don't have the space to keep. For outdoor gear and wear, instead of storing them in the basement, buy a chest that doubles in the entryway as seat.

You can get creative with your choices, but the key is to ensure that no clutter is left idly in your space.

#4 Apply the Simple Stick Rule

You won't be beating yourself or anything with this rule! The rule is this: you have to promise yourself that you won't buy **anything new** until you've removed all types of clutter from your house. (That means clothes, treats and other luxuries – not food!) You'll save money in the process and avoid cluttering areas with items that you really don't need.

#5 Make it a Habit

Bad habits are part of the reason why clutter rules in so many rooms. To get control, you'll need to break these bad habits by replacing them with good ones. Think about your bad habits and how they affect the amount of clutter you have. After that, choose one bad habit each week and do the opposite. So, if for example, you like to leave the phone off the charger, or your clothes on the bed, you'll do the opposite. Do this for the entire week until it becomes natural. The following week, choose another bad habit and change that also.

This may take some time to get familiar with - especially if you've grown used to the bad habits. However, if you work on clutter bit by bit each day, then you won't have a problem.

You can start living a clutter free life today. All you have to do is get a clutter collector in place, use the stick rule to prevent you from buying unnecessary items, and change your bad habits for the better. You'll be surprised how good you feel when you walk into a clutter free environment.

3

HOW TO CLEAN ANY ROOM AT LIGHTNING SPEED

Let's face it- it's not easy to find the spare time to clean every room in your house on a daily basis! Besides that, cleaning is rather time consuming and requires planning to get the work done. Believe it or not, you can actually clean any room quickly within the blink of an eye – yep, that fast, if you know what you're doing!

Step One: Get Your Materials Organized

Organization is the key if you want to save time when it comes to cleaning. To get organized, you need to first identify the areas that you plan to clean, and separate the materials that are needed in those respective places. If you take the bathroom, for example, you know that tub cleaner, countertop cleaner, window cleaner, tile cleaner, toilet cleaner and shower cleaner are needed. The most common cleaning materials would be sponges, rags, brushes and mops.

Collecting all the materials can be rather time consuming. However, if you manage to create a storage bin for each area then you can considerably reduce this time.

Step Two: Remove Visible Clutter

Visible mess - otherwise known as clutter - should be targeted first. If you start to work in the kitchen, then the visible clutter you may find include dishes on the countertops, excess pans on the stove, unused food products, small appliances etc. However, if you decide to start with the living room, then toys, books, and other paraphernalia are the most likely items that'll clutter such an area.

Step Three: Get Down to the Nitty Gritty

Now you'll need to find where dirt is located and get rid of it. Take care not to damage any furniture or valuable items in the process by ensuring you use the right types of cleaning agents for every item. Some 'all in one' cleaners may appear to be a cost and time saving wonder, but not if they damage the lacquer on your furniture or oxidize your brassware – always make sure you read the labels!

Try to use a good quality every day dusting cloth and a use separate damp one to remove dirt. Your countertops, behind the furniture and doorways are places to work on. After you have swept and dusted the entire house bring the vacuum cleaner out to clean the floor. If you're dealing with stubborn dirt then you'll need a mop and some cleaning agent to remove it.

Always clean the floors at the same time when you're cleaning more than one room in your house. This makes the process a whole lot easier and faster.

Tips:

Do similar tasks at once. This saves time and energy, and prevents mess during the cleaning process. You'll need to plan in advance to know which areas of your house you plan to clean and just exactly what you'll be doing. For example, if you decide to wash appliances, then do the same to the table and countertops. When you do this, you have a cleaner surrounding and won't have to plan another day to get this done. It will also save you lots of time.

Get your priorities in order. When you prioritize, you'll need to identify just what you plan to do. What exactly is your goal when you're cleaning? Do you want to clean some areas superficially to make them appear clean; or would you rather a deep clean approach?

When you prioritize, you'll focus on your primary goals and tackle those first. This will make your cleaning approach more organized and you'll get even better results. If you decide to do a deep clean in your kitchen, then this means you'll be cleaning the refrigerator, removing grease from the oven or stove or any other process that requires a good amount of energy. Deep clean in your kitchen does not include your countertops - this is superficial cleaning. When you establish your goals, you must strive to stick with them to avoid becoming sidetracked.

Get the right tools. The effectiveness of your cleaning depends on the tools you use. You need to do some planning to identify which tools you'll need and which you already have. Check your supplies to ensure you have enough. This is to ensure that you don't run out of cleaning agents in the middle of a deep or superficial cleaning job.

When you arrange your tools and plan ahead, you'll save time and money. You'll also avoid becoming frustrated and stressed. Try to buy cleaners in bulk to save money or look for special sales that are being advertised for certain brands.

You don't have to take the entire day to clean anywhere. With some planning and the right tools, you can clean any room effectively in less than ten minutes. When you clean rooms quickly, you'll have more time later to do the things you enjoy.

4

PERSONALIZED CLEANING CHECKLISTS

You'll agree that cleaning and trying to keep your home clean can be a time consuming affair. However, believe it or not, you can easily take control of just how much time you actually spend cleaning, anywhere! This is possible through a checklist that outlines the step-by-step cleaning processes in a systematic fashion.

There are other benefits to having a checklist. The main one that stands out is that it makes it easier for the clutter creators (your spouse and children) to clean up the storm they leave behind. When they are presented with a structured checklist, they won't be overwhelmed by the task and neither will you.

Step One: Make a List of Your Plans

Do this for each room on a separate sheet of paper. For example, if you decide to separate the garbage to remove the recyclable items, then the ideal checklist will be.

- On Monday morning separate the bag from the recycling container.
- Place the contents into large recycling bin
- Take the bin to the pick-up-point
- Put another bag in the recycling container
- When pickup is complete return the recycling bin to its original location

Assess all the rooms in your house and make a simple list of what needs to be done in each. After that, prepare a detailed list in the same format above to have a structured order.

Step Two: Order is Key

Before you clean anywhere it is important to identify the logical order that is involved in the cleaning process. For example, if you decide to clean the refrigerator in the kitchen, you certainly won't use the same rag to clean off spots on the floor. Each area should have its own cleaning material, whether it is a cloth, a sponge, mop or brush, to avoid contamination.

The same applies if you decide to clean the bathroom. You can clean out the shower, the bathtub and the sink all at the same time. If you decide to stop and dust the medicine cabinet or sweep behind the sink then this will create some degree of disorganization. You want to increase your own productivity when you are cleaning, to save time and get the job done faster. To get this done, simply order your tasks on your checklist in a manner that is most efficient and increases your own productivity.

Step Three: Scheduling is Important!

You'll need to know when you intend to clean a certain area the house. You can make an estimate of how much time it will take and include this beside each step on the list. When you put a schedule on your checklist you'll be able to plan just how many areas you can cover in one day, morning or afternoon. This improves your own efficiency and makes the whole cleaning process more productive. If you don't set time apart, then you'll find you may spend the entire day cleaning.

Time slots on the checklist also make it easier for your family to plan their activities. For example, if you children want to watch their favorite program at 8:00 on Saturday morning, they'll know that this won't be possible since you'll be cleaning. The same applies on your end - you'll be able to keep track of other things you like doing and just how soon or late you can get involved after you are finished cleaning.

Step Four: Make it Organized

It's easier to scribble your checklist on a little piece of paper. However, avoid doing this and turn to a professional word processor instead. Your list will be a lot more organized when this is done, and the presentation will also be better.

Create a bullet point list to make your checklist easier to understand and better organized. A good word processor usually has the option to create bullet points or numbered lists. The key is to make your checklist clear to understand and be organized. Do this for each of the rooms in your house and save it in folder.

Print the lists. These lists will be around for a long time, so you'll need to protect the surfaces. You can either laminate or put them into a transparent bag. You can use a dry erase marker to make it easy to keep track of your progress. To share the chores, place the list in a visible area in the house, so that everyone can see it and partake in making the house clutter free.

Step Five: Download Your Free Checklists

Every reader of this book is entitled to free Gleam Guru home cleaning checklists and planning lists, totally free of charge! Just head over to **www.gleamguru.com/GOFREE** and sign up for the newsletter to download and utilize them straight away.

5

THE ESSENTIAL THREE-TIER SYSTEM

Some people just can't seem to get their organization right. They place labels to identify different things. They go to great ends attempting to get organized, but at the end of the day everything is still chaotic!

If this sounds like something that you're going through, then you'll definitely benefit from the three-tier system.

What's involved in three-tier system?

Many organizations use the three-tier system to get their operations back on track. The system forms the foundation on which they organize tasks, or deal with clients that they have. The main corner stone that makes the three-tier system a success, is the level of priority involved. By prioritizing, you're able to organize tasks better and maximize your own efficiency in the process.

First Tier

The items you use on a daily basis are known as **first tier**. Personal items that fall under this category may include keys, shoes, handbags, watch, etc. Items in your office and home that can be considered first tier can include your computer, pencils, paper, phone charger, etc. In the kitchen it would be your utensils, cookware, refrigerator and stove.

The more you use first tier items the easier it should be to find them. This is only possible if there is a specific location created for them. When you do this, then you'll know where to look first and won't lose any time in between. You should choose a location that is accessible. It should also be handy, thus making it easy to place and remove things when you feel.

Second Tier

Items that are not used with much frequency are known as **second tier** items. They can be used either weekly or even monthly, but not on a daily basis as with first tier items. To fully understand these take your entryway for example. Your umbrella is a good example of a second tier item. If you move to your home office, then it can be your printer and business plans. In the kitchen it would be the toaster, fryer, popcorn popper and other appliances that are used infrequently.

These types of items don't need to be accessible since you rarely use them. They also don't need to be out and visible as with first tier items. This doesn't mean that they should be hidden and difficult to find. Your umbrella, for example, in the entryway doesn't need to be overly visible. You can easily store such an item in a bin for raingear or even in your hall closet. They key is that you really won't need to use them frequently, so immediate accessibility is not that important.

The same rule applies for items in your office. Your bank statements can be kept in a file cabinet that is next to your desk. They're not visible, but are accessible when you need them.

In the kitchen, appliances that aren't used often can be stored in an out–of–the-way cupboard or a pantry. You should choose areas that you won't need to access on a regular basis to store these, so as to avoid going through them to get to what you want.

Third Tier

The **third tier** items are items that you rarely use and when you do it's usually on a special occasion. These can be items you use once or twice during the year. It can be that special door decoration or wreath in your entryway. It can also be a family will or income taxes, in your home office. Your cake stand, fine cutlery or special holiday tablecloth are considered third tier items too.

You don't need to have these three tier items readily accessible. They can be stored in areas that are rarely used to avoid cluttering areas that you use more often. Closets, bins and other low profile storage areas are some examples of where they are usually placed. You'll need to use proper labeling and keep them in a logical order, to ensure that they are readily accessible when you want them.

You can improve your organization today by adopting the three-tier system highlighted above. Simply ask yourself: are my items organized in this manner or are they stored away in an illogical order? If you decide to change how you've been organizing things, then you'll find you will optimize the use of your space, and will be more efficient with your time. This helps to prevent clutter and having to constantly reorganize your house to find what you need.

6

CREATE ERRAND, EVENT & CHORE CHARTS

You'll find just how easy organization can actually be when you and you're family have a central information station. You can call this station your Command Central. You'll need to consider your family's unique characteristics, demands and needs. If you're not sure how to get everyone to fall in line, then use the great tips below to create event, errand, and /or chore chart that's ideal for everyone.

Information Board and Post-Its

Simplicity is usually the best solution. Create a calendar by using a piece of poster board in a color that complements your wall. Draw six rows and seven columns on the sheet by using a ruler. Use a permanent marker to write the days of the week in the seven columns. This is a very simple and yet effective charting process to create a calendar.

Ask your family what's their favorite color and buy posts-its in that color. You'll use both large post-its and small ones to get the job done. Small post-its on larger ones are a good option. You'll write the days of the month on the large post-it.

Think about what each family member will do and write it on the post-it. Place this at the proper date. This is a very cost effective solution to keep track of chores in any household. You can easily change the post-it as situations change and update the empty slot with new information.

You can use different colors to represent various achievements. You may even consider using a deduction system. This will encourage everyone to be consistent, so that they don't lose points. A red post-it could represent deducted points. If, after the end of the week, someone has a large number of red post-its under his/her name, then you can assign more duties the following week. This is more like a punishment system that will stimulate everyone to do their chores to avoid being given more tasks.

To be fair, you can also use another post-it to represent "chore relief". This works in the same way as the punishment system just that instead of punishing you'll be rewarding them with one less/different chore in the following week. This will give you the opportunity to alternate chores between different family members.

Chalk board / White board

You can choose to either buy a white board or make your own chalkboard by using chalkboard paint. Try to place it in an area that you're children won't be able to erase it easily. If you manage to do this, then you'll have another effective low cost system to track chores. Simply use different dry color markers or chalks to distinguish each family member.

If you have children, you can draw cartoon shapes on the whiteboard or chalkboard. Each shape will only be awarded when they do their chores. If they accumulate the same number of shapes after the end of the week, then they'll get a certain number of points. You can use the shapes to grade whether the chore was done well, poorly or satisfactorily. A smiling face for example could represent a job well done, whereas a serious face, a job poorly done. Simply get creative and imaginative with what you think will work best with your family.

Desktop Calendars

Desktop calendars are also handy. You can find these at your local office supply store. They have all the months of the year on pages that are easy to manage. They also provide enough space to write all the information you need. This is a great system for a small family. Choose the main living area in your house to hang it.

Manufactured family organization systems are another excellent solution to consider. First check if this type system is right for you and your family, before you spend your hard earned money. The poster board or chalkboard systems are perfect, if you have a constantly changing schedule.

You can add some fun to the tracking system by using rewards, stickers, shapes, and fun colors. Little children simply adore these - and some adults too! Use stickers to reward your children each time they do their chores. When they manage to add up a certain amount of stickers, then you'll surprise them with an even bigger treat, like going to the movies, shopping or another exciting treat.

This type of system is perfect for children of all ages. Older children will learn how to be responsible by adding and managing their events to the family calendar independently. Smaller children on the other hand will learn the benefits of being responsible and doing so as a family.

7

SECRETS OF ORGANIZED FAMILIES

Does your family seem to be struggling while other families around you are shining with triumph? You'll be surprised to know that those families may not necessarily be as happy as they appear. Chances are, they have some organization secrets up their sleeves.

A few things that they know are:

Individuality is Important

Children love to feel a sense of ownership and belonging. Do your children feel this in your home? Before you answer this question, think about the situation with individual space in your home. Do your children have their own space to hang their belongings? They may have their own bedroom, but do they have a designated area for their personal belongings? If they don't, then you can easily solve this problem by providing a cubby in the entry way or mudroom for their belongings. An individual coat hook is another great option to ensure that children have a place to put their shoes, coats and bags.

A family caddy is another solution if your children are old enough to have mobile devices. You can use labels to ensure that each child has his or her own individual space and genuinely feels that it is his or hers. When you do this, you eliminate the fuss and fights between siblings, since they won't need to feel they have to compete with each other to get their own space. They will also not feel sense of jealously, since you'll be treating each equally by giving them the same rights.

Command Central

It's not easy to keep track of everyone's schedule. However, despite the challenge you can easily create a central calendar that makes it easy for the entire family. This will be known as a Command Central. It will be the area that everyone goes to to understand what needs to be done and when. You can easily integrate it with your chore chart to make tracking more straightforward. To do this think about:

- Preparing a desktop calendar and hanging it on the wall so that everyone can see it. Make sure it is accessible to everyone—even small children.

- Getting a calendar. You can use a chalkboard or white board calendar to make it easy to write and add changes.

- Using a Google calendar. This is a great way for you to teach your children computer tricks. Small children may not be able to accompany the steps involved in preparing a calendar, but older children can. Get them to prepare their Google calendar and then integrate it into the central family calendar. You'll need to give your children Internet access to do this.

- Using creativity through colorful post-its. This is an excellent option if you have children. Simply designate color-coded post-its for each child and day. You can then write what you wish and explain the rules and requirements of each code to them. Try to keep it simple, so that it is easy to remember.

You don't necessarily have to use post-its, if you don't want to. Try to find a solution that works best for you family and that makes the central command area effective in getting their attention.

Daily Outline

A daily structure is perfect to get your family organized. It also makes it easy for everyone to know what to expect and plan their lives around it. Your children will also benefit from it, since they'll be fully aware of the outline and the requirements. A well planned daily structure will ensure that children do certain tasks at the same time each day. This means that they wake up, eat at a scheduled time. You should also ensure that they watch television only after they have done their homework. All of this information should be included on their daily schedule. Other aspects to take into consideration include getting their chores done at the same time every day. They must also go to bed at the same time daily as well. With this plan in place, you'll get your family organized in no time. Your family will also have more time to relax and rest during the day.

Your family's organization needs will change as situations change. Always bear this in mind to avoid stress and unreasonable requests that can cause friction in your family. It's also important to realize that no family is perfect and that as each member gets older adjustments have to be made. The system you create should make it easy for your family to step back and relax.

8

THE TEN TOOLS EVERYONE NEEDS TO GET AND STAY ORGANIZED

You'll need to know how to strike the balance between organizing yourself and your life. Too many tools and the whole process can get time consuming and confusing. Too few tools and you'll need to actually find solutions that work. Here are ten tools you need to know to get and stay organized.

#1 Planner / Calendar

There's no secret to this one. (The only secret is actually using your planner and not just preparing one!) Better results are only guaranteed if you use your planner on a consistent basis. You can explore various types of planners to actually find one that works for you. Some of the common planners can be prepared on paper, computer and even mobile device. Just ensure that the one you choose fits your needs and personality.

Avoid getting cluttered by using planners for different purposes. For example, you can separate your business planner from your personal planner and so on. The important point to take into consideration is to ensure that the planner actually works for you. If you find that you can integrate all on the same system and get effective results, then by all means go ahead.

#2 Clutter Collector

Many items become displaced on a daily basis. If you don't have a system to collect and replace them where they belong, then you run the risk of cluttering specific areas. This is where the clutter collector comes in. You'll simply place it at a strategic point in a location where you move around frequently. Once or twice a day, look around you and identify items that are out of place. Place these items in the collector.

You should ensure that these aren't items that you'll use frequently. After a week or less remove the items from the collector and place them where they really belong. This system helps you in two aspects: in getting organized by removing clutter and also being conscious of what you actually taking. With the latter, you'll think twice about removing an object without replacing it since you'll want to avoid the extra work next time.

#3 Media Command Center

Create a media command center to get your DVDs, remotes and other media items organized. You'll place all media items in the command center to avoid chaos and broken items. This will make it easy to find them, when they aren't being used and also to end any frustration you'll feel trying to remember where you placed them. Consider storing DVDs and other media in a box or drawer to guarantee easy access.

If you need to remove your media on a frequent basis, then try using a box or some other storage container to place them. This is very handy if you move media from one room to the next. To prevent them from becoming lost in other items, place them in an organization box. There are special bags and wallets at the book store for media items such as DVDs and CDs. Think about getting a few of these to better organize your media items, according to your preferences.

#4 Phone/Electronics Command Center

Phone recharging can become a nightmare of chaos in the middle of tangled cords, wallets and keys. Everything gets all jumbled up and if you aren't careful can break or damage caddies, cords and phones in the process. Thanks to innovation, you don't have to settle for this.

Some caddies can house up to five mobile devices. These are perfect to avoid the confusion. You'll need to create a single location for these rechargeable items to avoid getting other items jumbled with them. The cords on the devices can labeled to guarantee even better organization.

#5 Cleaning Baskets / Storage

Cleaning supplies shouldn't be jumbled together. To avoid this, use a basket for each area in your house and place the respective cleaning items in it. For example, you'll have a basket for cleaning items for the kitchen and another one for the bathroom. This system is perfect for household areas that require a lot of cleaning.

#6 Chore Chart / Family Organization Area

Trying to keep your family organized requires planning. This is why it's so important to have a family organization area. This area will make it easy for everyone to know what needs to be done. You can use post-its on a large calendar to create a family organization area. When your needs change, simply remove and update the post-its accordingly.

#7 File Cabinet

Your personal information should be stored in a file cabinet that's fire proof. You can organize the file cabinet according to the type of document you have. Bank statements, tax and other personal documents should be stored according to their category.

You may also scan these documents to have digital copies of each file. You'll be able to find portable scanning devices on the market to do this. Frequent back-ups will be necessary if you decide to store them on your computer.

#8 Task List

Make a list of tasks that you need to complete. Do this on a daily basis and at the end of the day check to see what you've accomplished. The task list can be pen and paper, mobile device or any other convenient option. The key is to ensure that it is readily accessible when you need it.

#9 Binders

Information that's used often should be stored at convenient points. Binders are great for storing this type of information. You can use three ring binders to store just about anything. Some common items to store there include recipes, schoolwork to even receipts.

#10 Minutes, Minimum, of Free Time

Clearing your thoughts is also important to guarantee organization. This isn't necessarily a tool, but it plays an integral part of organization. Take some time each day to reflect and get your thoughts organized.

9

TIPS FOR KEEPING YOUR FAMILY ORGANIZED

Keeping your family organized isn't an easy job. Not only do you need to think about your children and spouse, you also need to think of yourself as well. Knowing what to do and when to do it is an important part of being organized. Read the great tips below to know how you can keep your family and everyone else organized.

Start with Yourself First

You can only keep track of everyone else and yourself if **you** are organized. Think for a second about what works best for you, and choose the most effective option. If you believe that the traditional pen and paper will work, then use them. If you think that a day planner or computer calendar is right up your alley, then use those. The key is to use a solution that you can access and update on a consistent basis. Organization is about being consistent, so make sure you not only plan, but also do.

Create Personalized Solutions

Assess each family member and try to identify his or her strengths and weaknesses with organization. This will make it easier to create individualized solutions that work. Always remember that each person has a different personality, some are thorough in everything they do, while others aren't. For example, if your son is good at organizing his toys, but always seems to put them back in the wrong places, then his problem is the identifying where to put them. Work with him and try to find ways to encourage him to put them in the right location.

Different organization systems can achieve the same results or even similar. Accepting this makes it easier to appreciate each individual's organization choice. For example, if your daughter is structured, then she may keep a calendar on the wall with all her meetings, practices and homework. If your son is more relaxed he may keep a calendar in his iPhone and get message updates about each item. These are two different systems, but they can work for each child.

Create a Central Zone

A central information zone makes it easy to keep track of tasks and organization goals as a family. The type of tool you decide to use to achieve this will depend on your objectives and what works best for everyone. A monthly calendar on a poster board is a good idea worth trying.

Post-its can be used to keep track of each day. You can use color code post-its to make it easier for each family member to better identify with the requests. When they look at the poster board and see a particular color, then they can tell directly what's happening and how they're involved. This will also help to reduce any resistance to your organization plan.

The information at the central zone must be clear and simple. Try not to place too many post-its on the board (if you decide to use a board), because a cluttered look can lead to confusion. Prepare a table and complete it with the name of each individual and their color. That way, it is easier to keep track and remind each other about what needs to be done.

Individual Space

Everyone in your home will need his or her own space to feel some sense of individuality and avoid disorganization. A perfect place to start would be the entry way in your home. If each person doesn't have areas that is his or hers at this location, then things will become disorganized. Your children may come from school and just dump their belongings on the floor. Your spouse may leave the keys on the table, in the couch or anywhere else that seems available at the time. This all leads to disorganization, because at some pint everything becomes muddled together. Things are also more prone to get lost.

Create a space for everyone to avoid reliving the above scenario on a daily basis. Use good, practical tools that are effective in getting results. At the entry way you can use a coat rack. You may also want to think about a shelf or baskets. Use labels, and teach your family to put their things in their space. The same rule applies for you and your spouse. You can also ensure things are never lost with charging stations.

The same "own space" concept can be applied to any room you chose. This includes the laundry room, bathroom, and living room. Each area can have individualized storage space that makes it easy for everyone to keep track of his or her items. It is also a great way to teach children about the importance of organization.

Get yourself organized first, before you start with your family. Organizing and keeping your family organized is a challenge, so you need to be prepared. Create organization systems according to each family member's personality. This makes it easy for them to relate with the system and eventually accept it. Finally, look around your home to see the best place to create individualized space. Get the necessary tools to make this possible and apply labels to identify each family member.

10

HOW TO HELP CHILDREN GET ORGANIZED

Children won't know anything about organization until they are taught. As a parent, you'll need to teach them all the details to ensure they get into the habit and take it with them into adulthood. No matter the age of the child, you can still teach organization skills. Here's a list of useful tips to make your job easier.

Young Children

Your children can learn about organization through their toys. Your role will be to create places for their toys and teach them why it's important to put them back in place. It may be necessary to use different tools to ensure that you get your message across.

You'll need to consider your child's age as well. If you child cannot read yet, then use shapes and whimsical drawings to motivate them to be organized. For example, if you have a young child that loves block games, then you can use a box with a picture of a block on it. Whenever the child sees the box with the block, then they'll know what to do.

Teaching your children to put their toys away doesn't have to be a battle! You can make clean up time a game that they learn from and enjoy. You can use just about any game, but it's important that your child responds and interacts. If he or she isn't responding to the game, then alter or change it entirely. A good example would be to challenge your child to put their toys away. You can use a timer to add some excitement to the challenge. Some children will literally burst with enthusiasm as they try to beat the timer. To make it even more exciting, use a reward system. For example, your child can get to watch a movie, play a game or help with baking cookies.

Younger School Aged Children

Prepare a calendar for your child when they start to go to school. This will help them to become organized and to better deal with responsibility. You must bear in mind that homework, getting to school on time, and other school activities should be part of the calendar. The earlier you start doing this, the easier it will be to get them to respond to more responsibility as they get older.

Prepare and post the calendar on the wall in the main living room. Use coded post-its to make it easier for them, or any other tool you find useful to help them to keep track of their schedule. A good example of teaching your child responsibility would be to include a 30-minute break to watch their favorite TV show after homework. With this example, you'll teach them to get the important things in life completed first, before they move onto something else.

Participate in your child's life and get them involved in the calendar preparation. Ask them about their plans, school obligations and write this on the calendar. It's important they feel they're a part of the preparation because it makes the calendar more personal. It will also teach them to get in the habit of learning their own schedule. This way, they will be responsible for what they do to fulfill it.

Older School Aged Children

The older a child becomes, the more responsibility he or she will have to undertake. Your role as a parent will be to teach them the importance of systems, to ensure they know how to prepare and complete their schedule without feeling overwhelmed.

The organization skills you teach your child should help them to organize their schoolwork. Additionally, they should be taught how to organize their material so that they do not miss homework, and should always have all they need to study for tests.

Next to systems you'll need to teach your child the importance of follow through. It's important that they know this to ensure that they get results from their planning and systems. For example, your child may prepare an excellent system to track homework, but if they don't use it or know how to apply it, then it will become ineffective. You'll need to identify the areas that your child will need more help.

It's necessary that the proper guidance, materials and support be provided to your children. They must learn to be independent with little input from your end. If you bail them out then they do not follow through, then this defeats the purpose of teaching them about creating systems and consequences. They must know that once they miss an assignment, then there will be consequences.

As a parent, you'll need to be a good organization role model to ensure that your children have a reference point. It won't be easy teaching them organization skills, but it is nonetheless an important part of their lives. They will take the lessons into adulthood and how they respond to organization then, depends on what you teach them now.

11

STORAGE SOLUTIONS FOR YOUR HOME

Homes that lack space will quickly become disorganized and full of clutter. This is a problem that can be overwhelming if you have a lot of things to place in the little space you have. Here are some solutions worth trying to create space in your home.

Storage Solutions in the Living Room

The living room should always be organized to make it more welcoming. Next to the kitchen, it's the only room where the family congregates to do activities together. To avoid clutter and guarantee organization, consider:

Dual-purpose furniture - Try to buy furniture that has extra storage space. This way you don't necessarily need a storage room and can still keep items out of sight. For example, a coffee table that has enough storage space to put small items. Or an ottoman that you can use to store seasonal things, such as, party decorations, special tablecloth, etc. These are all good ideas that allow you to optimize the space you have.

You can also use shelves in the living room. This is a more traditional solution, but is quite effective in storing small and large items. There are dedicated shelves on the market that you can consider for your specific needs. Media centers with extra shelves are also a solution.

The key here is to find a storage solution that is effective and that complement your room. It is also best to store items that are only for that specific room. For example, storing utensils in the ottoman in your living room may not be a good idea if the kitchen is not nearby. You can also consider using bookcases to store items and keep your living room clutter free.

Bedroom Storage Solutions

Personal items and linens can be stored under the bed quite easily. This is a very useful area to even store large boxes or other large items that you rarely use. You'll need to measure your container to ensure that you get the right fit. Frequent vacuuming will be necessary to prevent dust from accumulating on the surface of these items. Try not to force any container under your bed just because it appears just a 'little' too big. Any bulges can damage the mattress over time. So, it's ideal to have a little gap between the container and the bed.

A shoe organizer and dual-purpose furniture are two other alternatives for storage in your bedroom. Small items that can easily clutter your room, such as ties, shoes, and belts can be placed in organizers that are designed specifically for them.

Kitchen Storage Solutions

The kitchen is one of the most used areas in any house. You'll find that it's easy to get messy and cluttered. The extra space is needed if you like to entertain guests. Storage solutions for the kitchen include canned food organizers. These organizers can be placed in your pantry and cupboards.

They are perfect for storing canned foods and soda. You can maximize space and efficiency by taking advantage of space saving spice racks. Get valuable cupboard space by placing pans and pots on decorative racks or hangers. This is especially important if you rarely use these items.

Around the Home

Look around the house to identify possible storage areas. A good place to start would be under the stairs. This is usually a wasted area that is rarely used. Also, ask yourself, how are your closets being used? Do you think it's necessary to have more shelves, or would buying storage containers be enough?

You can use armoires to separate different spaces. These are perfect in your basement. They can also be used to separate your workspace and laundry room. They will divide the room and provide storage solutions in the process. Use decorative bins to get even more storage space.

Think twice before you throw containers out. Sometimes they can be used as storage items instead of buying new ones. For example, food containers can be used to place the remote control, keys and even storage containers. An old cookie jar is perfect to store small items. You can use it in the laundry room to store any little trinkets you find after emptying pockets.

Look around your home and think about the possible ways you can optimize storage space. Try to identify ways to make the storage space better and also possible solutions that you can implement.

Further Reading

As home storage is such a huge topic to cover, you may be interested in my second book, '**Store This! Simple Home Storage Systems**' also available from Amazon.com.

12

TIPS FOR AN ORGANIZED ENTRY WAY

Your entry way is the first area people will use to judge your house. To create a good impression, it must reflect your personality and should be inviting. Making the most of this opportunity could even determine if your guests are likely to visit again in the future! Here are some useful tips to help you get your entry way organized and welcoming.

Remove the Clutter

Your entry way must always be clutter free. Remembering this will ensure that you have an inviting entry way 365 days of the year. A cluttered entry way will create a very bad impression and leaves guests and even you overwhelmed with the many items that are competing for little space. This is certainly not the effect you want to create in your home sweet home, now is it?

Look at the entryway and determine what is really necessary and what's not. Items that can be removed should be stored in areas where they do not cause clutter. Try to find ways you can even decorate your entryway to add character to it. When you're removing clutter or decorating, always maintain simplicity at the focal point. The simpler, the better able you'll be to create a warm inviting effect in your entryway.

Storage Solution and Space Must Sync

Large storage solutions can be used in large spaces. For example, furniture with different compartments is perfect to place in spacious areas. You'll be able to store as many items as you wish without worrying about creating a separate space in your house to do this. Just get furniture that complements each aspect of the room that it will be in. This way you can't go wrong.

An armoire is an example of the ideal option to place in an entryway. If your entry way is large, then a large armoire means that you'll be able to store umbrellas, boots and many other personal items. However, if you have a small space, then large furniture is not ideal. Instead you can use small furniture with various compartments to store different items.

Change Habits

When some people enter their homes, they simply drop everything anywhere they feel. They leave their shoes at the entryway, keys on the nearest table they can find and other belongings in a chair or the sofa. If you are like these people, then you'll need to change your habits. Firstly, you'll need to separate somewhere for each specific item. The place you chose should be accessible.

Your coat for example can go on a coat rack and your shoes on a shoe mat. Each location can also be decorated to reflect your specific style and tastes. They don't have to be brash to make a statement, but simple and functional.

Create Character

Your entry way should have character and not be dull and traditional. You want people to enjoy the experience of walking through it since it is the first impression they'll get of your house. You can use just about any decorative tool to make it unique.

Artwork and mirrors are perfect to make it feel personal and unique. You can finish the look with the right light. Use lighting that is sophisticated, soft and not too bright. Your visitors should feel the effect of the decoration from the minute the step into your house, to the instant they are guided to where you want to take them.

Add Charm with Color

The color of your entry way is also very important. You can choose light colors or bright colors. If you go with bright colors then you'll need to ensure that it is not overbearing. You can also find ways to tone it down by using storage bins and even a bench. These should be lighter color. If you decide to use wall art, try not to overdo it.

Many homeowners go with a yellow entryway. This is an excellent option, if you are thinking about creating a clean effect. You can finish the look by using whimsical designs and accent pieces that add charm to the location. Bright pillows on your bench are another way to add more character to an entryway that's painted in a light color.

Your entry way should be empty when you are remodeling. You'll be able to see the space you have and evaluate what you can do to make it better and more welcoming. Note each of your ideas on paper. When it's time, select the best one or combine ideas.

13

KITCHEN ORGANIZATION TIPS

Planning and hard work are necessary if you want to organize your kitchen. One of the biggest problems is that most people have more kitchen gadgets than they actually need. If that's you, then read the tips below to get your kitchen organized with quick easy steps.

Create Zones

Kitchen countertops and workspaces are generally used for certain tasks. Your island may be used to organize your food preparations, whereas your sink is used for washing and draining food. Your tools should be appropriate for the job they are doing. For example, you should have spoons and knives near to where you prepare food on your countertops.

When you create zones you are able to organize how each area should be. You're also able to plan what tasks should be performed in each. This makes it easy to organize things and there are less chances of creating clutter. For example, if you know that your countertops will be used to prepare food, and then you'll get all the necessary appliances and gadgets in place near to that area.

Reorganize Rarely Used Appliances

Your kitchen may be full of rarely used appliances that are simply taking up space. If that's the case, reorganize your storage by putting appliances you use more at accessible areas. The ones that you don't use often can be placed in storage areas you don't need. You may even consider doing a yard sale, or giving your excess pans and pots to charity, to free yourself from clutter.

You may also consider replacing your old appliances with ones that have double duty performance. For example, an appliance with all-in-one function of a vegetable peeler and a blender. This will reduce your storage space and leave you with only appliances that you need. You'll also be more efficient when preparing food since you have one appliance with two different functions.

Drawer Organizers are Assets

The problem with having too many utensils is that you rarely find what you're looking for. Somehow, the utensils you don't really need take up a lot of space and those you need are nowhere to be found. This can be irritating especially when you're preparing a meal and need a specific utensil to finish the job. You can solve this problem with a utensil holder.

The utensil holder will feature the utensils you use on a regular basis. The others that are rarely used can be stored in a utensil organizer. This will create more space in your kitchen and eliminate the clutter. Try to get holders that will separate your utensils according to type and shape.

Space Saving Storage

Many innovative storage devices are on the market now. You don't have to stack items on top of each other to create space since they are already built for this. For example, a can rack is perfect if you have a lot of canned food. You'll be able to store many more cans and you'll be able to eliminate a cluttered shelf and free up more space. Look around in your cupboards and kitchen to see which items are predominant. Take a trip to your local dollar store to get products that are specially made for these items.

Keep it Clean

It's important to have a system plan in place to ensure your kitchen is always kept clean. A clean kitchen gives a welcoming feel. It's also motivating which means that you'll want to keep it squeaky clean for as long as you can. Your system can be based on doing certain tasks each week to keep different locations in the kitchen clean.

You don't have to spend hours trying to organize your kitchen. Assess the space you have and evaluate all the items that are in it. What you don't need, throw out, plan a yard sale or give to charity. What you do need, try to find out if there are dual appliances with the same function.

It may be overwhelming at first trying to remove clutter from your kitchen. You'll need to ask yourself, what you really need and imagine how your kitchen will look and feel if re-organized. Home design software on the market can give you a good idea about what to expect if you reorganize your kitchen. This is a versatile solution that allows you to play with different configurations until you are fully satisfied. You'll get to see what your kitchen will look like and make adjustments accordingly. With these tips you'll be able to keep your kitchen clean and organized.

14

LAUNDRY ROOM STORAGE SOLUTIONS

Next to the basement and attic, a laundry room is usually a very cluttered area. Often. little regard is given to organization, since it is a room that is rarely used. It's also not uncommon to see a windowless closet or a poorly installed wire shelf or two hanging off a wall. These dismal features add to the disorganization that is quite common in a laundry room. The good thing is that it's possible to keep this room organized with some planning.

Unsurprisingly, most people don't want to spend time in such a disorganized room. As a result, the clutter increases and the room is rarely organized in any worthy sense. After some time, clean clothes get mixed up with dirty ones and baskets of clothes remain in the laundry room for ages. With a little effort, it is possible to organize the laundry room and transform it from a room of chaos to one of clean clothes and organized baskets.

The Essentials of a Laundry Room

When you walk into a laundry room you'll notice some basic essentials. These include laundry detergent, baskets, washing machine, drying racks, ironing board and an iron.

Homes with a large laundry room have all the necessary essentials. They do not look cramped since there is enough space for each item. In addition to this, people are usually more inclined to keep them organized. A small laundry room can become cluttered and disorganized in a blink. To avoid this, it's necessary to do some brainstorming to identify the best solutions to maintain an area that is organized and clean.

Your laundry room does not have to look dismal. You can consider adding some colorful painted shelving instead of simple old shelves. You may use a small storage bin to keep all the essentials of a laundry room organized. That means, you'll have a basket for laundry detergent, one for stain removal items and another for softener.

You can have a custom made cupboard installed to add a different look and feel to the room. The surface of the dryer does not need to be plain and simple. Get a decorated covering and place it over it when not in use. You can use this surface for folding. This will eliminate the need to open the ironing board to do this. The custom cupboard you install can be used to store small laundry room essentials and even the drying rack and ironing board.

Your hamper can be housed in your cupboard. This will add more storage space to your laundry room. You'll be able to store your dirty clothes there if you want. It's also important to consider getting a trashcan to place trash you'll remove from pockets. It can also come in handy to place lint.

You can find these cupboards at your local home store. They are usually located at the cabinet area of the store. It is also important to look at the kitchen cabinets. You need to get the perfect size for your laundry room to ensure that you do not create a cluttered feel when you install it. A floor cabinet is a good option if you do not have a large laundry room.

The Fun Extras

You really don't need to do a lot to transform your laundry room. By simply painting the walls you can create a welcoming feel. You can consider adding an entertainment set to make it easier to want to be in a laundry room. It is one of the few rooms that are rarely visited by family members unless they have to wash something or put their dirty clothes in the baskets. Your laundry room can be modern and more inviting by installing a small flat screen television or MP3 player. No matter how simple the gadget, the effect in the laundry room will be felt immediately.

A dismal laundry room is something of the past. The depressing look and feel are also passing scenes that anxious people like yourself want to change. You can use simple storage solutions that are inexpensive to make your laundry room more attractive and appealing. This will eliminate the cluttered space and make the whole room more inviting to do basic laundry services and other tasks.

Use simple cabinetry to get additional storage space too. These can either be mounted on the wall or remain on the floor. Your choice will be based on the size of the laundry room. With a splash of color and media you can make any laundry room more modern and inviting.

15

STRATEGIES FOR AN ORGANIZED HOME OFFICE OR DEN

An organized home office will make it easier to manage your finances, make decisions and find important information. This is an important area in your home and should be kept clean and free from any type of clutter. A chaotic home office that is disorganized, makes it impossible to get your finances together and other important tasks that need to be accomplished. It becomes even more critical to ensure this area is kept clean if you are running a home-based business and meet clients there. Here are some tips to make your home office neat and tidy:

Know the Purpose

The purpose of your home office will define the layout. It is important that it suits its purpose, to ensure that it is organized accordingly. For example, your home office should support your home-based business if that is the aim. However, if the layout is for family organization, then business support is not ideal.

When you define the purpose of your home office, then it becomes clear what you'll actually need to accomplish this. This will assist you when organizing and making relevant decisions about the layout and how you should keep it clean.

Organize with a Tier System

Working with and having the right tools in your home office is essential. If you're not able to find important tools, then things become chaotic and counterproductive. A tier system eliminates the chance of this happening. With a tier system you'll store the items you use frequently close at hand. The items you use less frequently are stored within reach. Those items that you rarely used can be stored in boxes and kept in areas that you hardly access.

An example of the last item can be last year's taxes. You don't need these items on your desk or within your working space since they cause clutter. To prevent this you store them at convenient locations that you can access when you are ready.

Everything Has A Place

This can be a simple rule if you know what you are doing. However, for most people it does not work, because of the system they created. A perfect example of this would be the in/out box.

The in/out box theory is plausible, but the setback is that an inbox can become quite full very quickly. Many of the items in it do not follow an organized pattern. As a result, it will be overflowing with disorganized piles of paper. This system is inappropriate for someone that does not have the habit to clean out his or her box on a daily basis. They may start off initially doing so, but eventually lack the follow through and begin to let things pile up in their boxes. Only someone that is in the habit of cleaning out his or her box can work with such a system.

You'll need to know what type of person you are. Take some time to think about this by identifying your habits and personality. It's always best to work with your habits instead if trying to radically change them. Think about the frequency you access your box. If you only do so once per month, then it's best to get several boxes. You'll then be able to create a storage point for each item you believe is important. Whether it is for your taxes, receipts or any other item that you can think of.

Group Electronics

Cords are items that you'll find in any home office. They can become entangled, disorganized and unsightly. The main culprits are your phone cords, printer cords and computer cords. There are many other electronic and media devices that you use in your home office that can add to this large bundle of entanglement. You'll need a single location to place all of your cords to eliminate the possibility of having a cord clutter. You may also use cord-hiding solutions or cable wraps if you want them to be discreet in your office.

Labels Are Important

Labels are perfect to keep your documents organized. They also help to make it easy to find things. However, labels can become ineffective if they do not provide enough information. This increases the likelihood of disorganization and chaos. For example, if you have a file labeled "RECEIPTS", this information is not enough to know what types of receipts are in the file. They can be supermarket receipts, utilities receipts, bank receipts, or speeding ticket receipts. You'll need to add information that explains the type of "receipts" in the file. Use a tier system to distinguish the importance of each receipt file. For example, create a file labeled "receipts" and then separate files for each type of receipt you have. Your labeling should be clear and make it easy to find what you need in less than a minute.

You don't have to force yourself to change in order to organize your home office. Work with you personality and habits. Create systems that will allow you to accomplish your goals within your limits.

16

CONCLUSION

I f you follow the steps outlined in this book, I promise you will soon be on your way to a clutter and stress free home.

Please take the time to review this book at Amazon.com, as I would love to know what you think, and how it has helped you.

Best wishes,

Colette

YOUR FREE GIFT

Keep updated with Colette's latest books online

twitter.com/gleamguru
facebook.com/gleamguru

Don't forget to visit The Gleam Guru to claim your free home cleaning checklists and planning sheets

www.gleamguru.com/GOFREE

3017884R00038

Printed in Great Britain
by Amazon.co.uk, Ltd.,
Marston Gate.